Makeba's
First Day of School

Anthony D. Amaker

To order additional copies of this book, contact:
Xlibris
1-888-795-4274
www.Xlibris.com
Orders@Xlibris.com

Chapter 1

It was two and a half hours later, that Makeba awoke to the silence of her house. She went to the bathroom where she quickly washed her face, and brushed her teeth with baking soda. She looked at her pretty ebony features in the mirror. Then she realized that she was indeed hungry. Just then she heard her mother's voice saying, "Makeba, Makeba, young lady it is time to get up for dinner."

Makeba opened the bathroom door, and came out to the kitchen to meet her father and mother.

She immediately got a giant hug from her father, who had not seen her all day. She then took her place at the middle of the table, and let out a tiny yawn.

"You must have had a busy day, my little princess?" her father asked.

Makeba just nodded a yes in affirmation as her mother brought out a basket of fresh fried shrimps and scallops to the table along with fresh tomatoes, lettuces, and cucumber salad. She followed that with bringing out a home-made, blue-cream cheese dressing, and a nice hot kettle of licorice tea.

Makeba's father started with the Nguzo Saba, they all sat down and enjoyed the meal with each other's company. However, Makeba could sense that this was not to be an ordinary dinner time meeting. She felt that her father wanted to express himself. Maybe it had to do with something dealing with the special new school, the shipping business, and her mother looking for work or her own business?

Right as her thoughts were completed in her little mind. Then her father began to speak, "Makeba so you have been down to the shopping mall called African Are Us? Well, that is just one of the many treats that are in stored for you."

"Your mother and I have been doing a lot of planning for you. We have outlined a new school for you, which we are sure you will enjoy. The times of the world are so hard on us, so your mother will have to look for a job."

"We only wish that we could have you learn of your heritage and Black History at home. At your age, your mind should be developed by your parents' guidance. We hope that you will enjoy this school, because we have searched really hard ever since your graduation party," her father stated.

"Father, will I have friends just as I did at my party, and will I enjoy games just the same way as it was at my party?" Makeba asked, with both bright brown eyes wide and worried.

"Oh honey, there are over 300 children enrolled in the school we have picked for you. It has over 25 teachers educated out of Howard University, Spellman, and

Morehouse Colleges. Therefore, you meet and be with over 300 children during your break time," her father answered her.

"We chose this new school over all the others because it teaches in the same manner, which both your mother and I would have taught you at home," he continued.

"I like to be taught and learn new things, just like we did when we went shopping today. I got to see an Ostrich from Africa. It is a bird, that is really big and runs on two feet," Makeba stated.

"That is very good my little princess, and while you were with your mother, did she explain to you about her looking for a job?" her father asked.

"Well, she mentioned it. But I wanted to go with her. I know that I cannot, that is why I have to start at this new school, right?" she replied.

"Right, it is only during the days, and once everyone gets home, we will have our open family talks after dinner. Now, Makeba there is nothing to worry about, because we love you and we'll make sure everything is just right for you," her father stated.

"Right now, you have a little over 14 days to get prepared and to learn with us. I know you will be ready, because you are a very bright and intelligent young lady.

There is a program on television that I want you to watch on the PBS station. It goes off right before your bedtime. Go watch it, while I have a few words with your mother," he stated.

Makeba dashed off to the room with the big screen television in the family room, but quickly took a handful of shrimps with her. She could hear her mother's voice call after her, "Makeba, do not forget to brush your teeth after you eat, honey."

So, Makeba made a quick stop at the bathroom before actually reaching the family room to watch the educational show her father wanted her to.

"Melody, I had just gotten home when I ran into an old friend, who has a shop downtown. Well, he is going out of business, and wants to rent the space for as low as $300.00 dollars per month. I know how much you like to sew, and make your own clothing for you and Makeba. Especially, how you like to design your own pattern for those satin, and silk dresses. Do you think you could open up your own business, and do your own thing for a change? This will be much better then working for someone else. We can apply for a small business loan or grant, and open up a business account at our local bank," Mr. Hakim expressed to his wife.

"Well, honey I did have some ideas about African bridal gowns for women, and even started some new patterns in the leather jackets and pants sets. I will be willing to give it a trial run," Melody replied.

"Well, I could give an advance on the rent of $600.00 dollars this week. Then I will put in some overtime on the boat, before Makeba starts school in two weeks. I will be able to help you on the weekends to fix up the place to your satisfaction. Are you willing to give it a try or what?" he asked her.

She slowly moved into her husband's arms, and hugged him with a kiss.

She said, "Whatever my king wants, he shall receive."

Meanwhile, little did Makeba know that she would be watching a community of the many animals of Africa; while her parents were living out of their many plans emphasized in the speech of the Million Man March. Learning to do for self, by opening up a small custom made tailor shop in the downtown area was a dream come true for Melody Hakim. Now things were beginning to look up for this African-American family.

Makeba's father would definitely make good on the $600.00 dollars advance for the shop by working overtime on his ship. The seafood market on the Eastern coast was growing, and next year he would be looking to expand his business. The market on Lobster, Crabs, and other shellfish, etc, was growing. It looked to be a wonderful year for his family in the 21st century.

Makeba was fascinated by the many animals she was watching on television. She saw Monkeys, Tigers, Lions, Elephants, Gorillas, and other animals. Some that she noticed were on the walls of the restaurant at "African Are Us". She knew that it was getting close to her bedtime, and the program was almost over. She knew that she would probably have very nice dreams about the animals and new school. She could not wait to have them.

Chapter II

For the whole next two weeks Makeba learned a new word, and its meaning. All she heard from her parents was the word preparation, and she knew that it meant to get ready. That is all she, and her parents did for the days to come.

Right after that night, that she had the dreams of all the beautiful animals from the continent of Africa. She had visited the lovely Nile River for herself, which had big Crocodiles. She saw all the big cats called Lions, Leopards, Cougars, Black Panthers, Tigers and Cheetahs. She was in the deepness of the jungles, and surrounded by trees. The trees had song birds of all colors, and the big bird from the restaurant called the Ostrich was in the dream.

Makeba stepped out of her dream, once she had heard her mother calling her.

"Makeba get ready, because we have to get downtown before one o'clock to pay the rent for the new shop," her mother said.

Makeba and her mother were going to visit the small shop, that she was about to rent to start her small business venture instead of working for someone else. When they got there, she realized it was bigger then a closet, that her mother had mentioned; that most of the sewing would have to take place at home. She was only going to be there to drop off the rent money, and do some quick cleaning up for now. Then they would come back on the weekend, and get it ready to open on Makeba's first day of school.

Meanwhile, Mr. Hakim was doing business to expand his small ships to obtain five more ships for the Atlantic Ocean. He was meeting aboard his ship, which is called "Fantasia". He was meeting with his brother Tayshawn, who ran a shipping fleet on the Western coast of the Pacific Ocean. He was sent by request of their father to look into the fishing business, and to make an investment on the behalf of the family. He and Mr. Hakim had spoken on the terms of the percentage, crew size and wages. This information would be needed to run an effective business on the Eastern coast.

Tayshawn stated, "Kwan, we are looking into expanding the family's business with further investments, and I have 200 men ready to work as long shore men as a productive crew. I have the money towards about five ships like the Fantasia, here."

"Well, brother I will be more than happy to help you in the investment of the maritime trade, and getting the family expanded in this market. I heard you, and Dad wanted to open up some Seafood restaurants as well. Is this also true?" Mr. Hakim asked his brother.

"Well, this is true, but it will be a trial run based endeavor. You will be the boss on this side of the country running things on your own end of the Atlantic coast. You will be paid an extra $1,000.00 a week to manage the ships and crew, which will be about 40 men per ship. In addition, we will provide you with 20 percent of the weekly catch of the fish for yourself," replied Tayshawn.

"How long are we looking at this kind of family partnership, and management of the crew?" Mr. Hakim asked.

"We have already arranged a 10 year contract, which you could sign or have your attorney look it over. I will be back in about one week's time, because we are opening some more restaurants besides the ones on the Eastern coast. I have to go visit our cousins in the South, and Midwest" Tayshawn replied.

"I will do that, and see you in about a week before we make good on the deal. In the meantime, give my sincere regards to Dad, and I look forward to doing further business with the family very soon." Mr. Hakim said.

Afterward, on the dock at the shore of the Atlantic Ocean some two hours later, Mr. Hakim was showing his brother some master fisherman skills. His thoughts were back on his business, which was now taking a new turn for the better. It was based upon the visit from his brother hearing good news. Such good fortune meant he would have extra money to further his daughter's private schooling and college education.

Back at home, Mr. Hakim informed his wife and daughter of the turn of events after dinner. Makeba took in all the new information that her father related to them. She too, had another busy day helping her mother cleaning up in the small shop downtown. As they finished she noticed that it was bigger than a closet after all. She wondered what her mother could have meant by making such a comment.

Makeba noticed that after the family discussion and dinner, that the family was still engaged in preparation. This kept everyone busy throughout the entire evening. She decided to work on one of her coloring books, which her mother had brought her sometime ago. When she finished with it, it was time for bed. For yet another new adventure awaited her, because she was starting her first day at the new school.

Chapter III

On September 7, 2004, Makeba woke up early at 5:30 A.M. before her mother. She was just so excited, for it was to be her first day of school. Her father was already in the shower before she could reach the bathroom, and he was coming out as she came to the door. He greeted her with a kiss and big hug. Then he asked, "Are you ready, sweetheart for your very first day of school?"

With a little shy smile she replied, "More then ever Daddy, but I am a little nervous."

`Then she ran into the bathroom to brush her teeth, and take a shower to get ready for breakfast.

Ms. Hakim came out from the bedroom, and greeted her husband just as Makeba finished her shower. She stated, "I am a little nervous about my opening day at the shop."

Then she too ran into the bathroom to get freshened up before preparing the family's breakfast.

"Well, honey knowing the wisdom, and grace of the Almighty, you will do just fine at the shop. Your talents are deeply rooted in your heart, and reflected in your culture," he replied.

"Well, as soon as I get out of the bathroom. I will prepare everyone a very good breakfast, and we should all leave together on time. It will be nice to take her to the new school together, and maybe that will ease some of her nervousness," she stated.

They planned to leave together, and drop Makeba off at her new school to start her new adventure in education. Mrs. Hakim had other things on her mind as well.

However, she concentrated on making a delicious breakfast of fresh squeezed orange juice, scrambled eggs with melted cheese on top with fresh tomatoes, onions, green bell peppers, on toasted wheat bread. She and her husband had some herbal teas of Saint John Wort, and gave Makeba a cup of Chamomile tea. They all sweetened their teas with the honey from the jar on the table as they ate their breakfast. She had placed fresh cut flowers from her garden on the table of both Roses, and Carnations. These brought a special color and brightness to the table. It also left a lovely aroma in the air of the dinning room.

Melody and her husband had just listened to the news to check on the traffic situation on the road before setting out to drive Makeba to school. It seemed that there was never anything good on the news these days, but the Hakim family has a bright new beginning on the horizon. Ms. Hakim had just completed five new African styled bridal gowns to place in the storefront window, which was on one side of the shop. On the other side of the shop she had some leather suits prepared for the younger customers. She had stocks of leather pants, jackets, silk blouses, robes, sweaters and satin shirts in her inventory. She had purchased a sign to read: "Ms. Hakim's Custom made tailored Wear and Gear."

Finally, Makeba would get her first look at the new school, and be away from her parents about six hours a day. They entered the car together, and fastened their seat belts. They owned a Audi Sedan, which was a dark blue color. She sat in the back seat, and rolled down her window to take in the view of the neighborhood full of lovely houses in different colors. Some were A frame style, and other were average two story family houses. It was only a half an hour ride to the school. As Makeba was taking in the rows of the Maple trees, and Oak trees, which made lines outside of most of the houses. She heard her mother speak to her.

"Makeba, this may be the only time to enjoy our company on the way to school. We have made arrangements for a school bus to pick you up at seven o'clock each morning throughout the week," she said.

Most of the way Makeba was in silence, and wondered what her first day of school would be like without her parents' presence. Just as she completed her thoughts, they pulled up next to a great big gray building that looked more like a castle to her. Before they would exit the car there was something father wanted to express to Makeba.

Mr. Hakim asked, "Makeba, what is the seventh principle of the Nguzo Saba?"

Makeba said, "Imani, it means faith to believe with all our hearts in our people, our parents, our teachers, our leaders and the righteousness and victory of our struggle."

Mr. Hakim replied, "That is absolutely right. Now, you see that building over there? Well, it used to be a mansion that belonged to a great leader of education. A former educator Dr. Woodson. It has now been dedicated to the growth, and development of young minds such as yours. The teachers in there are looking for your best benefit in the future, and that starts right now. Once you enter the classroom, the teachers receive the same respect as me and your mother. They are to take our places, while you are in their care for six hours a day."

They started to exit the car, and Makeba's heart was full of renewed joy for she was about to experience yet another field of education. It was also full of anxious ambition of the unexpected. "The New African Mind" was the sign that she saw above the school, which was seven stories tall. Seven was a cardinal and universal number she would also learn of in the school. Once you enter the classroom, the teachers receive the same respect as me and your mother. They are to take our places, while you are in their care for six hours a day. This school starts at pre-school level and continues to highschool level."

After they exited the car together, and walked towards the entrance of the school. It had two great big double solid oak doors with shining brass doorknob. The building had a look of granite of darkened gray and had several statues outside the main entrance.

Mr. Hakim rang the doorbell and waited for a moment, until a security guard dressed in a brown suit with beige strips on the sleeves and shoulders appeared. He had a brown matching captain hat with stars, and on both side of a seven. As Makeba's parents addressed him, they were allowed inside. They were briefly sent to the Principal's office on the third floor, which they had to all ride in the very large elevator with red carpet on the floor with a glass mirrored ceiling. They notice that the lights came through the side of the upper part of the walls, which were made of oak wood panels. After the meeting in the Principal's office, they all walked to Makeba's class. Mr. Shahid was the Principal's name, and he called the matron on the intercom to escort Makeba and her family to the classroom on the fifth floor; where she would eventually meet her teacher, and the rest of her classmates.

They all gave her a kiss, and hug before departing. She was told to be good and take care of herself and have fun. They then took the elevator back downstairs and departed their own separate ways to work. Makeba bid farewell to her parents as they left her standing at the classroom door.

MAKEBA'S FIRST DAY IN CLASS

Chapter IV

The matron introduced herself as Nisa, and Makeba likewise introduced herself back as they walked to the classroom door number 512. The class was conducted by a Ms. Salaam, who looked to Makeba to be about her mother's age, and size. Ms. Salaam was dressed in a multi-color gown from head to toe. It was green, burgundy, black, and gold kenti colors. She wore a turban of an African head dress styled, which covered all of her hair. Makeba noticed that she was also wearing sandals on her pretty brown feet, and her toes were brightly painted in a shade of lime green, which made her feet very noticeable. She took Makeba by the hand after a very short exchange of words between herself and Nisa.

They entered the room together looking very beautiful in their different colored gowns. They both looked like two beautifully dressed African queens, and they stood at the center of the class as Ms. Salaam introduced Makeba to the rest of the class. While she was doing so, Makeba was busy looking around at all the different pictures that graced the walls of the classroom. Ms. Salaam said, "Attention class, we have a new student, who I want you all to take time out to introduce yourselves to her during the break time. Her name is Makeba Hakim. She is from the Kushite community on the other side of town not far about 30 miles away from here."

"Well, Makeba please find a seat, and make yourself comfortable. Each desk is prepared with a lesson, a pen and papers. We were just learning the alphabet in our own style to enhance our memory as best as we can to reflect the true culture, and traditions of the African motherland," she told her.

Makeba made her way to the small row of seats, because the class was not very big. There seemed to be about 20 students in this one class. The chairs were all nicely cushioned and had a firm straight back for proper posture. The desk was open for her to place her personal things, which she would need or use during the school hours. Now it was time for the learning to begin for Makeba, and she could not wait. At the same time, she could not take her eyes off of all the pictures in the room. There were animals with the alphabet next to each of them. Then there were the picture of famous Black people, which she remembered seeing some of them before in a book her father read to her once.

Ms. Salaam went to her desk, which was made of solid oak, and brought out some cards from her drawer. Makeba could notice that every card had a picture and an alphabet on it. Ms. Salaam addressed the class, "Now, we are going to learn the alphabet in a very special way, and you will be tested. As we go over the alphabet I want you to trace the letter as it appears to you on the papers on the desk."

Makeba looked at the sheets of papers, and she remembered how her mother had shown her these same images in the house as she would read books to her.

Ms. Salaam took the first card, which has the shape of a skull and informed the class. "This is the continent of Africa. It starts with a letter A. I want everyone to trace the letter that appears first on the paper in front of you. Then to follow the next letter after I go through all the cards," she said.

Makeba and the rest of the class followed her instructions carefully.

"Now, the next card has a picture of a monkey with a long curled tail, and is on all fours bent over. It had a long dog like muzzle. Now class, this is an African monkey called a Baboon. I want you to trace the next letter, which is a B. B is for Baboon," she stated.

Everyone did as they were instructed, and Ms. Salaam continued to go through the entire deck of cards with pictures on them.

"Class the next letter is a C, which stand for Camel. This is an animal from the Northern desert region of Africa, and Asia. They used it for its milk, and meat. It also used for traveling over great distances, because it retains water and food in the two humps on its back." Ms. Salaam informed the class.

Makeba took notice of the brown looking animal on the card. It appeared to have sleepy soft eyes, and was covered in fur with big feet and a short tail.

Ms. Salaam pulled out the next card with a Dolphin on it. "This is a mammal that lives in the ocean called a Dolphin. D is for Dolphin, which is a highly intelligent mammal who swims in the ocean. He has helped man on several occasions." Ms. Salaam stated.

The picture showed a clear gray bottlenose Dolphin on it with a white belly. It had a waterspout on the top of its back to help it breathe.

The next picture was a huge animal called an Elephant.

"Now class, this is one of the largest mammals next to the whale. It is an African Elephant," she continued.

The picture showed an animal with a short tail, and two big long tusks sticking out of the side of its face. It had a long nose called a trunk, and its skin appeared to look wrinkled.

The next picture she brought out was of a Falcon. "This is a Falcon, which is a bird of prey. It hunts other birds and small animals. This is a very special symbol to the ancient people of Kemet, which is the original name for Africa. It represents the son of Isis, who was named Horus by the Greeks," she stated.

Everyone traced the next letter in line with the other letters. F was for the word Falcon, which Makeba would later remember.

The picture shown on the next card was a small animal that looked exactly like a little mouse.

"This class is a Gerbil which is a small mammal that lives in the desert of Africa. Some people keep these small animals as house pets in cages nowadays. G is the letter that stands for Gerbil," Ms. Salaam told the class.

Everyone continued to repeat the same and tracing as before. By the time the class would be completed Makeba's hand would probably be tired, but would be well worth it to her.

Makeba would learn twenty six letters of the alphabet, and twenty six new words would be added to her vocabulary. After the word Gerbil she learned the following.

"Now class, this animal right here is called a Hippopotamus, which is a large mammal found in the riverbanks of Africa. It received its name from the Greek explorers, who invaded Africa. They called it a river horse, because despite its very large size it can move very swiftly on land and lives during most of the day in the water. The next letter is an H, which stands for the word Hippopotamus." Ms. Salaam continued to instruct the class.

"This is a piece of land right out of the Southeastern part of Africa, and this is what is called an island. An island is a large or small body of land that is completely surrounded by water on all of its sides. This island is also a country called Madagascar. The next letter in front of you is an I, which stand for Island," she told the class.

"The items on the card in front of you are called Jewels, which are Diamond, Rubies, Sapphire, and Emeralds. The continent of Africa is rich with these items, which causes a lot of foreigners to invade the land of Kemetic people. These items have been both a blessing, and a curse to the people of the land. The letter J stand for the word Jewels." Ms. Salaam told them.

"The next picture here is a castle, which could be called a palace. This is an old representation to the ancient kingdom of Kemet. The land of Kemet is in the Northeastern part of the continent of Africa, which it is called nowadays. However, there were major beautiful kingdoms in the ancient countries of Egypt, Ethiopia, and Sudan. This is the land of the Kushite people, who ruled most of the continent along with parts of Asia, and Europe all the way up to the island of the United Kingdom. The letter K stands for the word Kingdom." she informed the class.

"Does everyone see this map of the country on the card? Well this is a country called Liberia, which is located in the Northwestern part of the continent of Africa. This was a country first established by freed slaves from North America, who returned to the motherland. Right now, there is a lot of controversy concerning this small country, but it should serve as a model concerning the movement of the Pan African theory of the Honorable Marcus Garvey. He is pictured over there in the back of the class next to the founder and contributor of the school. The letter L stands for the country Liberia. It represents Liberty, which is something we are all striving for as a people to gain, and show independence," she continued to inform the class.

"Now class, I have another map of a country not too far from Liberia. It is the country of Mali. It used to be one of the greatest learning centers of education on the continent of Africa. This was at a time when Africa was at its height of excellence, and the leader in education for the entire world. People came from as far away as Spain and Arabia to this learning center. We must establish as a people here in the America our institutions to reflect the ancient society of Mali's cultural integrity. The letter M stand for Mali," she told them.

Makeba did not know of any of the places on the cards. At this time, Ms. Salaam put down the cards on her desk which she had just used for the class. Then she started going around the class to check on the work of her students. Makeba wanted to ask her some questions, but told herself to wait to see what the teacher would do next.

Ms. Salaam instructed the class that there would be a small break time for the morning, and she would serve them a snack prior to completing the alphabets with the class.

"All right everyone, we have some snack to give out, and I will answer any questions that may be in your little minds concerning the cards we just went through okay?" Ms. Salaam said.

Chapter V

The class was in recess for a small amount of time, which was about 30 minutes for refreshments. Ms. Salaam asked everyone to be seated in the back of the classroom. For the first time Makeba noticed just how big, and spacious the classroom really was.

"Everyone, please take a seat at the tables for the morning break recess. Then afterwards we will finish the alphabet." Ms. Salaam told the entire class.

The back of the classroom was another room all to itself, and reminded Makeba of her own dining room at home. There were four tables, which seated four people each. At this time Ms. Salaam handed Makeba a name tag, which would allow everyone else in the class to remember Makeba's name. She noticed that everyone else also had name tags on. At the table with Makeba were Malik, Nkosi, and Sheba. Makeba thought to herself that she would probably meet the others later during the lunch time break.

Ms. Salaam went to a cabinet and retrieved several items from it, which Makeba could see clearly were fruits and bread. She went to a refrigerator and presented several pitchers of juice. From the cabinet she also had taken out some wheat bread and strawberry jam. She placed it on a second tray with some cream cheese, and fresh fruits. Makeba could see the delicious slices of fresh apples, oranges, pears, and grapes on the tray being prepared by the teacher.

Ms. Salaam placed plates in front of everyone, and some cups for the juice was given to them all. She filled everyone's cup and Makeba could not make out what was the juice, that she was being given. Then Ms. Salaam informed the entire class of what kind it was that they were going to drink with their snacks.

"Class this is Mango nectar, which I brought especially for this day and this class," she informed them.

Each table had its own separate pitcher, and tray with all the goodies. Makeba thought to herself that the food looked delicious, and she definitely enjoyed it. Then she noticed that no one at the table was speaking at all to one another. Then she heard Ms. Salaam tell them.

"Well do not be so shy with one another, because you all share the same destiny. You all came here to learn. So at least everyone can introduce themselves at each table," she told them.

All at once Makeba could hear everyone starting to speak, and she heard Malik introduce himself to her, then Sheba, and finally Nkosi.

She replied, "Peace, I am Makeba Hakim."

Then she looked at all the pictures, and asked Sheba a question concerning the one that interested her the most.

"Sheba, do you know who's that picture of over there?" she asked.

She pointed to the man with the captain hat on his head, who was in a horse driven carriage. He was dressed in a form of military style uniform, she also noticed.

Sheba responded, "Oh that is easy, that is the most famous Marcus Garvey. He was the pioneer of the back to Africa movement in the early 1920's."

Nkosi added, "Yes, he was a great African conscious person, who is often not given his full credit for the Pan-African movement. He owned his own ship line to take people from this country back to the continent of Africa, but he was also a businessman. He was eventually deported back to his original country of Jamaica, and brought up on false charges of tax evasion prior to that by the U.S. Government."

"Well, I never knew all that about him Nkosi. Where did you learn so much about him?" Makeba asked.

"Well, my mother is a history teacher in African American studies at a local college. She always provided me with an abundance of information on African American history; especially during Black history month in February." Nkosi replied.

"He is not all that smart, because I had to tell him who the person in the picture over there was." She injected while pointing to another picture on the wall.

She was pointing at a picture of Noble Drew Ali, who was born before Marcus Garvey started his movement back in 1886 and returned to the essence of earth in 1929.

Makeba stated, "You did not know who Noble Drew Ali was Nkosi."

"I have never heard of him before today. I always find myself staring at his picture, because of that hat he is wearing on his head." Nkosi stated.

"That is not called a hat. It is a fez. It is worn by the Muslims, who are from Morocco. He is the founder of the Moorish Science Temple of America, Inc. He was one of the first Muslims of African-American decent to study aboard in a foreign country to learn Islam, and bring it back to North America." Makeba informed them.

She said, "I told you he was the first Muslim in America."

Then Malik stated, "I do not know about that, because my father told me Master Fard Muhammad was the first to bring Islam to America."

"Master Fard Muhammad was not born in America." Makeba informed him.

Then before a small argument could begin, Ms. Salaam appeared at the table. She provided everyone with napkins, and plastic knives. She placed a spoon inside the jar of strawberry jam. Then she left them to enjoy their snacks.

Chapter VI

After the meal was finished, Makeba and the rest of her classmates returned to their seats in front of the class. They cleaned all the tables, and threw out all the paper plates and cups. As Makeba remembered cleanliness was the best thing next to godliness. At this moment, Makeba noticed the style of the gown that Sheba was wearing, which was Maroon, Gold, Purple, and light Green. She was crowned in a purple turban and wore bright Gold sandals. Malik wore a nice custom made silk shirt with a Chinese collar which was burgundy in color, and matching silk pants with black stripes going down the front. He had a silver plated named buckle on his belt and his name was also on the back of the belt as well. It appeared to Makeba to be a walnut color. He completed his outfit with a pair of nice looking leather sneakers, which had his name on it to match the shirt and pants.

Then Makeba turned her attention back to the classroom appearance and the many pictures that surrounded it.

"Well everybody, did you enjoy your little snack and little break time this morning? We still have lots of work to get done for the morning. I would like to complete the alphabets before lunch time. Does everyone feel like they have enough energy to finish the alphabets today?" Ms. Salaam asked.

Everyone in the class answered in unison, "Yes Ma'am."

"Let's see, we left off at the thirteenth letter, and can anyone tell me what that was?" she asked the entire class.

Shaheem raised his hand and was called upon by Ms. Salaam.

"Yes, Shaheem, what was it?" she asked him.

"It was the letter M." Shaheem answered.

"Yes, it was M, and we are now up to the letter N. Does everyone see the letter N?" she inquired.

Everyone answered again in unison for the teacher. "Yes ma'am."

Then she went over to the desk again and picked up another set of her cards. This one showed a picture of another map, and then she picked up yet another one with a map on it.

"Now class, these are two different countries located on the Continent of Africa. This one right here is called Nigeria and this one is called Namibia. Right now, Nigeria is rich in its discovery of oil reserves, and it is modernizing its society to new level of change. It is one of the most stable and strongest countries on the Continent. It has been the focus of the African Union for helping of other less fortunate neighbors in the region. It is the most populous of all the countries in Africa. At last count it had to my knowledge approximately 142,000,000 people in the country. It is approximately half Muslims and half Christians. It has a very small minority of Animus. It is located in the central northern part of Africa and this other map shows the country of Namibia which is in the Southern part of the Continent. It is bordered by South Africa. It is attempting to aid itself in self independence since the struggle of creation of the African Union. Its population is of mixed ethnic tribes, and it is rich in minerals and gemstones." Ms. Salaam informed the class.

The next letter is O, which is represented on these four cards. It shows the four largest bodies of water that surrounds the earth. These large bodies of water displayed on these cards are called Oceans. O stands for the Oceans. This picture here shows the shape and size of the Pacific Ocean, which is 68,634,000 square miles. This next picture shows the Atlantic Ocean, which is the second largest body of water, and is 41,321,000 square miles. The third one is the Indian Ocean, which is 29,430,000 square miles. The fourth and final one is the Arctic Ocean, which is 390,000 square miles." Ms. Salaam said.

"I will explain to you at another time about the numbers this afternoon. I know that everyone is wondering about the numbers that I have just mentioned concerning the size of these bodies of water, and what it all means." Ms. Salaam stated.

That took the questions of wonder right out of the children's' little heads. All except little Nkosi, who immediately raised his tiny hand to be noticed in the class.

"Yes Nkosi, what is it?" Ms. Salaam asked him.

"I already know about numbers and their meaning. My mother taught me to count up to a thousand," he stated before the entire class.

"Well, that was very good. Then you can help me explain to the class later this afternoon. Would you like to be the teacher's assistant during the math part of the class?" she asked him.

"Yes," he replied. As he displayed his big bright smile, he showed his white teeth of pearls that shown through the well lit room.

Ms. Salaam continued with the class lesson of learning the alphabets. The class seemed very eager to learn as she went on with the letters and cards.

"Now this letter is P. It is displayed on this card with the picture of a papyrus. It is a long stem plant found in the Northern part of Africa in the waters of the Nile River. It was chiefly used to make paper by the ancient Kushite people and has been discovered in many of the Pyramids. It's called aquatic sedge, which means of a long solid stem water plant." Ms. Salaam explained to the class.

"The next letter is Q, which is represented by this figure on the card of a queen. It is noted that some of the ancient queens of the upper and lower Nile valley replaced some of the Kings. Some went so far as to put on beards and the royal crown of the King when ruling the empire. One such Queen was Natshapsut, who had a temple built in her honor located in Deir El Dahari, Egypt. Let it be known that you all come from royal bloodlines of Kings, and Queens of the ancient Kushite Empire. You have a rich history, which will be taught to you during this week by another teacher at this school." Ms. Salaam said to the class.

The entire room was in awe at the fact that they were descendants of royal African or Kushite people.

"The next letter that follows after the Q is called an R, which is displayed by this figure on the card. He is a King, but a famous ancient Ruler called Thothmes III of 1500 B.C. He was the mighty conqueror and administrator of far away places. His empire and power reached as far away as the Tigris and Euphrates valley, which is now the country of Iraq. He ruled from the coast of Somali, Armania, Kurdestan, Syria, Arabia, Nubia, Lybia, Babylonia, and Egypt." Ms. Salaam informed the class.

The faces of the children were amazed at the power of African rulers in the past. This was something they were unaware of living in today's society and watching television, which did not show such power coming from this Continent.

"The next letter here on the card is an S, and it s represented by the Sphinx. This monument is over ten thousand years old, and is said to represent Horus, the son of Isis. It represents the generation of man, and there is a riddle of the Sphinx." Ms. Salaam told the class.

She continued, "Does anyone know of the riddle or the Sphinx?"

Everyone all at once answered, "No."

"Well, the riddle goes like this. What animal walks on all four legs, then walks on two legs, and then walks on three legs?" Ms. Salaam asked.

The entire class looked very puzzled because they had never heard of, nor seen any such animal at their young age.

"Well actually they are referring to the three stages of development of man and woman. You see class; everyone starts out crawling as a baby on all fours. This is the first developing stages where we begin to take on the education of ourselves from our parents. Then as we start to learn we start to walk as you and I do right now. We walk on two legs from after we are one year old. We continue on throughout life, until we become well advanced in age. Once we reach old age, we cannot walk without the assistance of a third leg or cane. This shows the three stages of human development from our youth, middle age, and old age. This is the key and answer to the riddle of the Sphinx. Man in this monument is actually man in three stages of growth," she informed the class.

"This letter is a T, which is represented by the displayed picture of an ancient Temple. These temples exist throughout the Continent of Africa, but the most famous temples exist in Egypt. There are some in Ethiopia, Sudan and as far south as the country of Zimbabwe. This is the picture of the Temple of Luxor." Ms. Salaam informed the class.

"Now, we are up the next letter which is U. U stands for the Universe. Does everyone see this picture of all the stars in the Universe?" Ms. Salaam inquired.

She showed them a card with many stars in the Milky Way, and then she asked the class to participate in a little experiment.

"Everybody, I want your answer to whether or not you have been outside late at night with your parents?" She asked them.

"Yes." The entire class responded.

"Then I want everyone to close their eyes. I want you all to think of the time you all looked up in the night sky, and saw all the stars in the universe," she told them.

Everyone in the class followed her instructions and immediately closed their eyes. They started forming the vision in their tiny minds of all the pretty stars they had seen in the past. Ms. Salaam continued to inform the class in a small exercise of meditation.

"Now, can everyone see all the stars as tiny little lights in the dark sky?" She asked them.

"Yes, we can see them." The whole class responded once again.

"Well, I want you all to keep this image in your mind for a little while and concentrate on them and their beauty. Look at how they light up the night sky. Now, think of yourselves as bright little stars in the sky. I want you to imagine your little bodies as generators of energy giving off light because you are little stars in the universal family of oneness. Now I want you to hold this thought in your minds," she instructed them.

After about five minutes of this exercise, Ms. Salaam continued the alphabets after inquiring of the class as to how they felt.

"Class do you see this next picture which is of a Vineyard? The next letter is V, which stands for Vineyard. A vineyard is a planted roll of grapes, vegetables, or fruit on vines. We just had some grapes during snack time. Grapes are used in making wine or grape juice and vinegar. Right now, there is a company who owns a vineyard in South Africa, who is selling wine of different flavors to reflect different tastes of Africa fruits. Even such flavors as coffee are being produced. Well, everything made of wine is currently an adult drink and grape juice is made for younger people such as yourselves." Ms. Salaam informed the class.

"The next letter is W, which we have a picture of the Waterfall. There are many waterfalls in Africa. Some waterfalls are used to generate energy or electricity to provide lights to the homes inside the countries of Africa," she informed the class.

"How is everyone doing?" Ms. Salaam asked the class.

At this point she decided to take a brief walk around the class and examined everyone's papers. She noticed that everyone was doing fine, and their parents must have gone over the alphabets with them prior to the enrollment in school.

Ms. Salaam looked at the clock on the wall, which was a big globe of the world on the wall. She noticed that it was going on twelve o'clock and she wanted to conclude the last three letters with the class before sending them on another recess for lunch time.

"Now class we only have three letters left to write and go over. Is everyone ready to finish up for the morning?" She asked them.

"Yes ma'am." The entire class answered her.

"The next letter is an X, and this letter is represented on the card is a Xylophone. X is also used as an unknown or unnamed representation in math. However, I want you to think of the picture of this musical instrument, which was made famous by an African American musician who called it a Xylophone," she told the class.

"The next letter is Y, which stands for the symbol in the next card. This is a Yam, which is an edible root also called a sweet potato. People cook this vegetable in pies and little mashed potatoes," she informed the class.

"Now the last letter, which is the twenty-sixth letter of our alphabet is Z. Z stands for the picture on this card which is a Zebra. Zebras are animals found on the Continent of Africa and look like and are related to the horse family. They have black and brown stripes on a whitish body, and live in herds on the plains of Africa," she completed.

She looked around to see how everyone was taking the information in, and their expressions. Then she informed them.

"Everybody, when the bell rings in two more minutes, I would like everyone to place their papers on my desk before leaving the classroom. You have recess for lunch. Malik, I would like you to take Makeba to the lunchroom. Then show her the yard, and introduce her to the rest of the classmates," she stated.

At the conclusion of her statement, the bell rang and the class was over for the day.

Makeba thought to herself that she had learned a lot this morning considering everything they learned.

Then she got up and placed her paper on the desk of Ms. Salaam, and looked for Malik. She noticed that all the others in the room were moving towards the door. She was now ready for a whole new adventure at school, and looking to meet her new classmates and friends.

She now could not wait for the afternoon class to begin and she yelled out.

"Malik, here I am. Please take me around and introduce me to the rest of the classmates," Makeba said.

"I was just looking for you at the door and sure I would be happy to," Malik responded.

Then they both exited the class to begin walking and speaking on the way to the lunchroom hand and hand.

The End

About the Author

The author, Anthony D. Amaker, is an African American raised in the Williamsburg section of Brooklyn, New York. He grew up during the height of the civil rights era and has taken a special forum to the causes of the African American struggles.

He is now working on matters of self-esteem and development for Black children because they are truly our future. He has grown up with a strong mindset to foster ambition, goals and self worth in all the children that he encounters. He has been raised in a big family and believes highly in the process of family values. He hopes to spread a sense of joy with every book that's dedicated to the children of all ethnicity.

Printed in the United States
By Bookmasters